BLACK HISTORY

Community
and Identity

Dan Lyndon-Cohen

FRANKLIN WATTS
LONDON • SYDNEY

This edition 2020

First published in 2010 by Franklin Watts

Copyright © The Watts Publishing Group 2010

All rights reserved.

Editor: Tracey Kelly
Series editor: Adrian Cole
Art director: Jonathan Hair
Design: Stephen Prosser
Picture research: Diana Morris

Dan Lyndon-Cohen would like to thank the following people for their support in writing this book; The Black and Asian Studies Association (BASA), Marika Sherwood, Arthur Torrington, Joanna Cohen and Joanna Caroussis. Thanks also to the Lyndon, Robinson, Cohen and Childs families.

This series is dedicated to the memory of Kodjo Yenga.

Acknowledgements:

Allover Press/Rex Features: 25t. Nicholas Bailey/Rex Features: 8. Can Balcioglu/Shutterstock: 18b/g. John Berry/Imageworks/Topfoto: 18. John Birdsall Photos/PAI : 9t. Miles Boyer/Shutterstock: 30 b/g. Brooklyn Museum of Art, USA/Bridgeman Art Library: 10. Derek Cattani/Rex Features: 27b. Liat Chen/PYMCA/Rex Features: 39. Steve Davey/Rex Features: 5, 11t. M Dykstra/Shutterstock: 38 b/g. John Frost Newspapers: 33t. Richard Gardener/Rex Features: 36. William Gottlieb/Getty Images: 23b. Monika Graff/imageworks/Topfoto: 17. The Granger Collection/Topfoto: 15t, 15b, 29t. David M Grossman/Imageworks/Topfoto: 11b. S. Hanusch/ Shutterstock: endpapers. Hulton Archive/Getty Images: 12. Trevor Humphries/Hulton Archive/Getty Images: 29b. Image Source/Alamy: 31. Chris Jackson/Getty Images: front cover l, back cover r. Nils Jorgensen/Rex Features: 27t. Frantzesco Kangaris/Getty Images: 16. Kathmandu Photography/Shutterstock: 10 b/g. Kevin Knight/Corbis: 25b. David Lee/Shutterstock: 34 b/g. Ian Miles/Flashpoint/Alamy: 20cr. Norfolk Record Office, UK ref. 742X7: 14. Operation Cease Fire,Boston, USA: 30c. PA Photos/Topfoto: 19. Photonews/Topfoto: 32. Picturepoint/Topham: 22, 23t. Rex Features: 9b, 26b. Craig Ruttle/AP/PAI: 21br. Nina Shannon/istockphoto: front cover r, back cover l. Tom Shaw/Getty Images: 38b. Sipa Press/Rex Features: 13. 28, 34c, 35. Terence Spencer/Time & Life Pictures/Getty Images: 20cl. Mario Tama/Getty Images: 37. UPPA/Topfoto: 33b. Warner Bros TV/David L Wolper Prods./Kobal Collection: 24. © 2010 WUFOAM, www.wufoam.com <http://www.wufoam.com> : 21bl. Dmitry Yashin/Shutterstock: 26 b/g.

Every attempt has been made to clear copyright.

Should there be any inadvertent omission please apply to the publisher for rectification.

PB ISBN: 978 1 4451 8082 3
eBook ISBN: 978 1 4451 8083 0

Printed in Dubai

Franklin Watts is a division of Hachette Children's Books, an Hachette UK company.
Carmelite House
50 Victoria Embankment
London, EC4Y 0DZ
www.hachette.co.uk

Contents

Introduction   8

Black Britons and African Americans   10

Multiculturalism   12

Community leaders   14

Diane Abbott and Condoleezza Rice   16

Flash points   18

Overcoming barriers   20

Celebrating black culture   22

Black people in the media   24

Sporting achievements   26

Sport and community   28

Tackling gang culture   30

The legacy of Rodney King   32

Stephen Lawrence   34

Black role models   36

Diverse future   38

Timeline – Community and Identity   40

Websites and Bibliography   41

Glossary   42

Index   44

Introduction

'Who do we think we are?' is a question that many of us will ask ourselves at some point in our lives. Our identity comes from different places – family, community, beliefs, culture and language, among others. In multicultural, multi-ethnic societies people often have more than one identity. Labels, such as 'black British' or 'African American' are used to place people into simple categories. Here you will explore some of the people behind the labels.

Community roots

One of the ways in which identity is formed comes from the communities that people belong to. In this book, you will learn about the black communities in Britain, who have a history that can be traced back over nearly 2,000 years, and in the USA, with roots going back to 1619 when Africans were first brought to the colonies as

▲ *Dancers wearing costumes at carnival – when communities come together in celebration.*

indentured servants and later as slaves. You will also learn about the challenges that these communities have faced, the obstacles that they have overcome, and the contributions they have made to make these countries among the most successful in the world.

Heritage and identity

Identity is a very complex concept. There are many different black origins, and individuals define themselves in different ways. In London and New York alone, people come from countries as far-flung as Ghana, Angola, Somalia, Ethiopia, Nigeria, Jamaica and Trinidad – or have ancestors who do – yet all of them can be identified as 'black'. Many people of mixed heritage may also identify with being black, white, Asian or a mixture of backgrounds. However, what is important is how you choose to identify yourself.

◀ People, like those in this busy city centre, can choose to define their identities in many ways.

New voice

In January 2009, Barack Obama – who is of African and white heritage – was sworn in as the 44th President of the United States of America. This has given a clear message to black and mixed heritage people around the world that they can achieve and succeed in whatever occupation they choose.

Obama remembers his concept of identity as a child, growing up in multicultural Hawaii: *"That my father looked nothing like the people around me – that he was black as pitch, my mother white as milk – barely registered in my mind."* He also talks about the atmosphere of mutual respect of people from different backgrounds in Hawaii, which *"became an integral part of my world view, and a basis for the values that I hold most dear."*

▲ Barack Obama believes respect can help people live and work together.

Black Britons and African Americans

Over many centuries, there has been continuous migration into Britain, and as a result of the British Empire, people from all around the world live there. The USA has also seen many periods of immigration since the first successful British colony was established at Jamestown, Virginia, in 1607. The Jamestown colonists joined hundreds of Native American tribes (the original inhabitants of North America), who had lived across the land for thousands of years.

Black in the past

Archaeologists have discovered evidence of people of African descent living in Britain since Roman times. The Roman army brought African soldiers with them when they conquered England in 43 CE, and a Roman emperor – Septimius Severus, born in Libya in north Africa – died in York in 211 CE. In Tudor times, a settled African community lived in Britain. Queen Elizabeth I even attempted to remove some Africans from England in 1596.

During the Transatlantic Slave Trade, from the 16th to 19th centuries, many Africans were brought to England – often working as servants. However, it wasn't until the 1950s that significant numbers of migrants from the Caribbean arrived. The British government recruited many skilled Caribbean workers to fill job vacancies in new service industries, such as London Transport.

▲ *This Turkish sculpture from the 2nd century BCE is similar to later Roman ones.*

African descendants

Most African Americans are descendants of Africans who were kidnapped in western and central Africa and held captive as slaves in the United States from around 1619 until 1865. After the American Civil War (1861–1865), slaves in the South were freed (in the North, they had been freed earlier) and many moved to northern cities, such as Chicago and New York, to seek work. But segregation laws (enforced separation of racial groups) resulted in many African Americans living in poverty for decades. By the 1960s, the Civil Rights Movement, led by pioneers such as Dr Martin Luther King, paved the way for greater opportunities. New laws were passed restoring the African American right to vote, and banning racial discrimination in employment, housing, education and public places.

African heritage today

In the UK, the 2001 census found that 600,000 Britons identified themselves as black Caribbean and 500,000 as black African. These groups are very broad ranging, and do not allow for the differences between cultures within those communities. In the USA, Census 2000 found that 36.4 million people (12.9 per cent of Americans) identified themselves as black or African American. Of these, 1.8 million said they were black as well as belonging to another race or races. However, according to historian Henry Louis Gates Jr, up to 58 per cent of African Americans have at least

▲ *A crowded street in Britain. People from different cultures form Britain's diverse society.*

12.5 per cent European ancestry (equivalent to one great-grandparent) and 5 per cent have 12.5 per cent Native American ancestry. In addition, there is a small population (under 1 million) of new immigrants from Africa. These heritage mixes make the whole question of identity a very complex one.

▲ *Teenagers at an Italian pizzeria in New York. The USA is a melting pot of different cultures.*

Multiculturalism

Multicultural is a term often used to describe diverse communities living together, but people define 'multiculturalism' in different ways. For some, multicultural communities should live alongside and respect each other, as 'separate but equal'. Others say that different cultures should live together and learn from each other to increase understanding and tolerance. The challenge for all societies is to find ways in which they can integrate without losing their own identity.

The melting pot

In the USA, the concept of the 'melting pot' has existed for a long time, and is more like the second definition of multiculturalism (above). Native Americans were joined by settlers from Spain, Portugal, England, France, the Netherlands, Sweden and Russia between the 16th and 18th centuries; along with millions of enslaved Africans transported to the USA during the Transatlantic Slave Trade. In the 19th century, Irish people moved to the USA to escape famine. The 20th century saw Italians, Jewish refugees fleeing persecution in Eastern Europe and Nazi Germany, and Hispanics from Mexico, Central and South America coming to find work. The idea of the 'melting pot' is that all of these different communities have come together to form 'one America'. As the generations pass, immigrants become more integrated into the existing culture, and it is the turn of new immigrants to find ways to integrate peaceably and successfully.

▲ *New immigrants arrive at Ellis Island, New York harbour c.1900 – the first stop in their new lives.*

▲ *Muslim women in France protest after they were banned from wearing the veil (see main text).*

Did you know?

In the 1800s, the US government tried to create a 'separate but equal' society when they forced Native American peoples to live on reservations (parcels of land governed as separate countries within the US). Since many reservations were located on land unsuitable for farming, many tribes could not grow food or make a living. The result was crippling poverty. Today, although some Native Americans live in US cities, many continue to live on reservations, where unemployment is still rife.

The veil debate

France had a large empire covering many nations in Africa and Southeast Asia based on a system of 'direct rule'. People had to become French citizens and accept the philosophy of the French revolution: '*Liberté, Egalité, Fraternité*' (Freedom, Equality, Brotherhood) for all. This led to the creation of the French 'melting pot'.

However, more recently, this policy has caused controversy. The government banned people, such as teachers and students, from wearing any religious symbols. Therefore, crosses, skullcaps and headscarves (veils) in the workplace are forbidden. Some people feel that this goes against their civil liberties and conflicts with their religious identity.

Community leaders

One of the ways in which the voices of a community can be heard is through political action. Throughout history, many inspiring leaders have emerged from the black communities in Britain and the USA. Their importance lies in the pioneering work they achieved. These role models have often been spokespeople for change and equality, dedicating their lives to giving their communities a voice.

British pioneers

In the UK, the first black person to be elected mayor was Dr Allan Minns (born in the Bahamas), who became the Mayor of Thetford, Norfolk in 1904. The first black British mayor was John Archer, who became the Mayor of Battersea, London, in 1912. During his acceptance speech, Archer said:

> "My election tonight marks a new era. You have shown that you have no racial prejudice, but recognise a man for what you think he has done."

▲ *Dr Allan Minns, wearing his mayoral chain of office, c.1904.*

However, it was 70 years later that the first black Members of Parliament (MPs) were elected. In 1987, Diane Abbott (see pages 16–17), Bernie Grant and Paul Boateng were elected to the Labour Party. Since then, there has been little progress – in 2009 there were 645 MPs and only 5 of them were black. Based on equal representation of the black population (2 per cent of the UK is black), there would need to be 13 black MPs.

American trailblazer

Frederick Douglass (1817–1895) was one of the most important figures in US history. He became a leading abolitionist, women's suffragist, orator, author and statesman. Douglass was born a slave in Maryland, and learned to read and write from white children. He began to teach other slaves to read and was whipped by his 'owner' as a result. Eventually he

escaped to freedom in the North. His influential autobiography *Narrative of the Life of Frederick Douglass, an American Slave* (1845) was a huge success.

Douglass was famous for his speeches and views and, in 1863, he conferred with President Abraham Lincoln about the treatment of black soldiers fighting in the Civil War. After the war, he held several important political positions including President of the Freedman's Savings Bank, Marshal of the District of Columbia, and Consul-General to the Republic of Haiti (1889–1891).

One of Douglass' favourite sayings was: "*I would unite with anybody to do right and with nobody to do wrong.*" He was truly an original black American voice.

▲ *This early photograph is of Frederick Douglass, c.1847.*

Senate players

Only six African Americans have ever served as US Senators to date. The first was Hiram R. Revels, an outspoken opponent of segregation who represented Mississippi in 1870–71. The second was Blanche Bruce, Senator for Mississippi 1875–1881. There was then a large gap until 1967–79, when Edward Brooke served as Senator for Massachusetts. Carol Moseley Brown, who was the first female African American Senator, served for Illinois from 1993–1999. Barack Obama also served in Illinois from 2005–2008, when he was replaced by Roland W. Burris.

▲ *Hiram R. Revels, c.1870. Revels was also a clergyman and educator.*

Diane Abbott and Condoleezza Rice

IN DEPTH

Black politicians take part in perhaps the most direct route to changing people's attitudes and improving conditions for black communities because they take part in legislation (law-making). Two important 21st-century figures are Diane Abbott and Condoleezza Rice.

▲ Diane Abbot was born in London in 1953, and later attended Cambridge University.

Diane Abbott

In 1987, Diane Abbott became the first black woman to be elected to the British House of Commons when she was chosen as the MP for Hackney North and Stoke Newington. She has since developed a strong reputation, often speaking out on issues that affect the black community, and in 2008, she won the *Spectator* Magazine Speech of the Year Award. Since 1992, Abbott has also been involved in Black Women Mean Business, an organisation that she established to celebrate and support black business women.

Another important area that Abbott has focused on is education, particularly the underachievement of black students. Abbott set up an initiative called London Schools and the Black Child, which includes an annual conference to discuss issues relating to the education of black students. This has focused on areas such as increasing diversity in the curriculum and looking at reasons why black boys, in particular, have such a high exclusion rate from schools. The annual London Schools and the Black Child Awards ceremony celebrates the achievements of young black people.

Condoleezza Rice

Condoleezza Rice is a diplomat, professor and writer, and became the first African-American woman to become Secretary of State under President George W. Bush from 2005–2009. In this role, Rice tackled international terrorism after '9/11' – the 11 September 2001 attacks. She believed that promoting democracy in Middle Eastern countries such as Iraq would

prevent future attacks, and developed a Transformational Diplomacy policy to 'maintain security, fight poverty, and make democratic reforms' worldwide. Rice grew up in the 1960s in Birmingham, Alabama, and experienced first hand incidents of terrorism due to racial prejudice. As the Civil Rights Movement in the USA progressed, violence erupted – local black churches were blown up and there were bomb threats at Rice's school. But her family was determined that she would be educated to rise above discrimination: *"My parents were very strategic, I was going to be so well prepared, and I was going to do all of these things that were revered in white society so well, that I would be armored somehow from racism,"* Rice said.

▲ *Condoleezza Rice now lectures on political science at Stanford University, California, USA.*

Flash points

In the 1960s, new laws attempted to reduce inequality and improve community relations in Britain and the USA. These outlawed racial discrimination in education, employment and housing. However, today, areas of concern still include the underachievement of some black students, police-community relations and the high number of black men in prison.

Prison projects

In the USA, the prison population has tripled in the past 15 years and a disproportionate number of inmates are black men. Initiatives from organisations such as the American Civil Liberties Union (ACLU) and National Association for the Advancement of Colored People (NAACP) are campaigning to protect prisoners' rights and improve living conditions. The ACLU's National Prison Project has five lawyers, who represent 50,000 prisoners

▲ *Many prison projects focus on giving offenders the skills they need to get jobs.*

in 20 US states. They work to reduce overcrowding, improve medical care, and eliminate violence and abuse in prisons. They also work with community and education groups to reduce the number of men who are sent to prison in the first place.

The NAACP's National Prison Project was set up to help former prisoners return to normal

Did you know?

There are around two million people in prison in the US. According to the ACLU,

"On any given day, one-third of all African-American males are under some form of criminal justice supervision, and for black males in their twenties, one in every eight is in prison or jail."

life in their communities. It includes helping them to find work and to break the cycle of repeat crimes. The Project also helps former prisoners resume their right to vote – because of state felony laws, which prevent prisoners and sometimes ex-prisoners from voting, an estimated 13 per cent of all black men in the USA are not eligible to vote.

1980s riots

In the UK, black people in London, Bristol, Liverpool, Birmingham and Leeds were worried that police 'stop-and-search' powers were being used indiscriminately against them. This, mixed with the high unemployment of young black people, created a tense atmosphere that exploded in rioting in April 1981.

The Scarman Report investigated the Brixton riots in London and stated the need to challenge racial discrimination. However, little progress was made and disturbances broke out again in 1985. It wasn't until the Macpherson Report (see page 35), that many people felt the issue of racism was being taken seriously by institutions such as the police, schools and hospitals.

▼ *Police shield themselves from missiles during the 1981 riots in Brixton, London.*

Overcoming barriers

Before the anti-discrimination laws of the 1960s and 1970s, in Britain it was legal to openly discriminate against black people. In the USA, racial segregation laws that lasted until the 1960s meant that African Americans – mainly in the South – were not allowed to eat at the same restaurants or study at the same schools as white people. Despite these obstacles, black communities, individuals and organisations have achieved great success through schools, churches and radio stations.

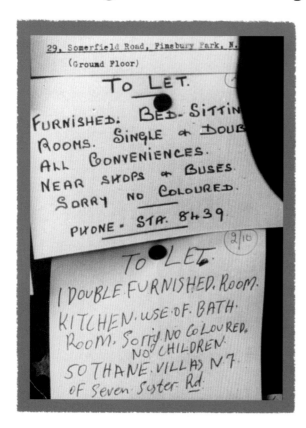

▲ Racist 'to let' adverts, like these from 1967, were a common sight in British shop windows.

▲ Black teachers, like this one, can motivate and encourage children from ethnic minorities.

Educational strides

Since the 1950s, one effective measure to boost the grades of black students has been the growth of Supplementary Schools in the UK.

These are after-school classes run by the black community for black students, and focus on a curriculum that brings black experience into the classroom. Lessons include black history, African and Caribbean culture, numeracy and literacy. This positive learning environment is important in counteracting the experience some students have faced in mainstream schools, where they have felt excluded from the curriculum.

Because children from minority communities often underachieve in urban schools in the USA, the NAACP has set up the Call for Action initiative. Under the scheme, highly qualified black teachers are trained and recruited to teach in schools with high numbers of minority children, where they serve as role models for children. These teachers have a better chance of directly encouraging children to go on to higher education at colleges and universities.

Community radio

With the emergence of digital technology, it is now possible to find a huge range of radio stations that cater for different needs. The contribution that black artists have made in the UK has meant that major radio stations from the BBC, such as 1Xtra, target black communities as well as a wider audience. Community radio stations provide an important opportunity to discuss issues affecting black communities as well as celebrating black music and culture.

In the USA, African-American operated gospel stations – such as WUFO in Buffalo, New York, founded in 1962 – as well as urban stations that play hip hop, R&B, jazz and soul – provide a crucial service for maintaining a sense of mutual support with others in the black community.

▶ A DJ at WUFO broadcasts music, news and community service and church group information.

Guiding hands

The Archbishop of York, Dr John Sentamu, believes in the responsibility of the whole community to guide young people to a positive future:

"We all have a responsibility to the young, not just to our own offspring or our families, but also to others. In Africa, there is a saying that 'it takes a whole village to raise a child'. There is little to be gained from looking at which council or social service is to blame when a young person is abused or abuses another. What of the parents, the relatives and friends? What of the responsibility of the local community who may – through fear – have looked the other way?"

Celebrating black culture

The celebration of culture and history is an important way that communities can grow stronger. In both North America and the UK, Black History Month encourages black communities and the wider society to learn more about black history. Festivals such as the Notting Hill Carnival in London, the multi-cultural Mardi Gras in New Orleans, and African American Heritage Festivals throughout the USA all celebrate aspects of black culture.

▲ Claudia Jones at the US embassy in London, 1963. She called for an end to discrimination.

Colourful carnivals

London's annual Notting Hill Carnival, which celebrates the music, dance and culture of the Caribbean, came from an idea by Claudia Jones (read more about her in the *Civil Rights and Equality* book in this series) and was first held in 1959. The carnival tradition came from Trinidad, where they were held to remember the abolition of slavery. By 1965, the carnival in London included parades and bands playing Caribbean styles of music, including calypso and soca. Today, it is one of the greatest street parties in Europe.

Mardi Gras (French for 'fat Tuesday') is the traditional French Catholic Carnival most associated with New Orleans. People from all cultures dress in colourful costumes, play music and party on the streets. The Mardi Gras Indians are African-American revellers who dress up in Native American ceremonial clothes. Dating back to the mid-19th century, this custom probably began as a tribute to local Native Americans who helped runaway slaves. It is closely linked with the New Orleans music scene, and

▲ *These people are on their way to a trendy party in Soho, London, c. 1950.*

Black History Month

The first black history remembrance was celebrated in the USA in February 1926, as 'Negro History Week'. Now called Black History Month, it is held in the USA, Canada and also in Britain since 1987. The aim of the month is to promote and honour black history, culture and personalities such as George Washington Carver (1864–1943). Carver was a US scientist, botanist and inventor who is most famous for researching useful crops for poor farmers, including peanuts and sweet potatoes, for which he found hundreds of different uses.

In Britain, Black History Month also aims to encourage a more diverse curriculum in schools. However, there has been some criticism, particularly within black communities, of Black History Month. Many people find it patronising and feel that black history should be integrated into the school curriculum, so that there is no need for separate studies.

many hit songs have emerged from this yearly tradition. In 2006, Hurricane Katrina caused devastation to the city, particularly the black community, but the Mardi Gras still went on as a sign of resilience.

Music legend

Nat King Cole (1919–1965) was one of the most important musical figures in US history. In 1956, the velvet-voiced singer and jazz pianist became the first African-American to host his own TV show, *The Nat King Cole Show*, featuring top stars such as Ella Fitzgerald, Harry Belafonte and Eartha Kitt in a celebration of black culture.

▶ *Nat King Cole fought racism all his life and refused to appear at segregated venues.*

Black people in the media

The way in which black people are represented in films, TV shows and the radio has a huge influence on the way people from other cultures perceive them. From being excluded and stereotyped in the past, the black community has grown to take part in these areas of the media, and many well-respected figures have emerged in the UK and US media.

'Roots' series

One of the most talked about TV programmes of the 1970s was *Roots*, a TV series based on Alex Haley's book about the Transatlantic Slave Trade. Over 100 million people in the USA watched the final episode, making it one of the most popular TV series in history. *Roots'* importance lies in the fact that it was one of the first times TV had shown black characters in roles that were created for them by black writers, which did not pander to the previous stereotype of black people being lazy, stupid or violent. In the first half of the 20th century, black characters often fitted into two types of roles – the 'minstrel', who was a talented musician, but was not very intelligent, or the 'mammy', a domestic servant who looked after children. *Roots* was a breakthrough for fairer representation of black people in the media.

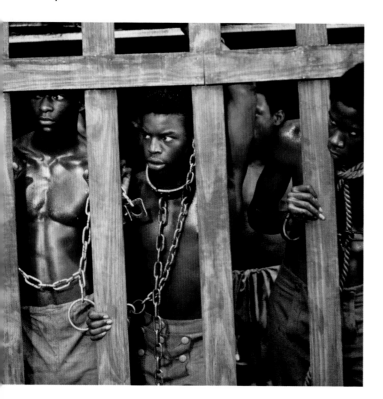

▲ *A scene from* Roots, *showing enslaved Africans wearing the chains of slavery.*

Growing influence

In the past, black people were often only seen in the media in sports and music fields, which limited opportunities for young people to see role models. Today, the visibility of black people in television, film and radio is much greater. In Britain, Lenny Henry – comedian, writer and co-founder of Comic Relief (a charity founded in 1985 to help the famine in Ethiopia) – has made a tremendous contribution to popular culture since the 1970s. In the USA, the actress, TV presenter and businesswoman Oprah Winfrey is famous

▲ *Oprah Winfrey was ranked the richest African American of the 20th century.*

Did you know?

In the USA, the annual NAACP Image Awards ceremony celebrates the outstanding achievements of black people in film, TV, recording and literature. Founded in 1970, the Awards work to break down stereotypes of African Americans in these 'visible' industries and encourage more realistic portrayals on screen. It also honours those who promote social equality through the creative arts.

for her own TV show – she is known as one of the most influential people in the world. However, there are still concerns at the way black people are represented on the news, which sometimes focuses more heavily on 'black on black' violence, gang culture and crime.

Role models

The increasing number of black musical artists and sports stars has led to a debate about the importance of good role models for young people (see pages 36–37). This is partly the result of the negative associations connected with 'gangsta rap' music, whose lyrics and videos often glamorise gun violence and gangs. The videos can also be sexist and homophobic, and send out the message that to be happy, you must acquire huge amounts of cash to spend on jewellery, champagne and fast cars. The media in Britain and the USA has focused heavily on gangsta rap, creating the concern that young people were aspiring to become gangsta rappers rather than doctors, lawyers, teachers or electricians, for example.

▲ *Many people believe that rappers do not necessarily provide good role models.*

Sporting achievements

Young people often shape part of their identity from the role models they admire, many of whom come from the world of sport. Modern sport in the USA and Britain features an abundance of very talented black players from many disciplines – from football and athletics to tennis, basketball, golf and more. Their stories and achievements excite and inspire people from all backgrounds.

Tennis royalty

Venus and Serena Williams are two African American sisters who took the white-dominated game of tennis by storm in the late 1990s while still in their teens. Mentored by their father, they trained hard and began playing tournaments at 10 years old. Since then, they have competed at prestigious tennis tournaments including Wimbledon, the US Open and the Australian Open. Each sister has been ranked No 1 woman player in the world several times. In autumn 2000, Venus and Serena represented the USA at the Olympic Games in Sydney, Australia, and Venus became the second woman in history to win a gold medal in both singles and doubles matches.

The Williams sisters have been responsible for bringing new athleticism to women's tennis, and for raising public awareness of the game generally. Venus sums up her and her sister's careers: "*It's been a journey. For women of colour, for my family. It's one dream coming true after another.*"

▲ *The Williams sisters celebrate winning the Wimbledon Ladies Doubles final in 2009.*

Olympic athletes

At the 2008 Beijing Olympics, the black sprinter Christine Ohuruogu became the first British athlete to win a gold medal in the 400 metres. Ohuruogu joined a distinguished list of black British Olympians that includes Daley Thompson, Linford Christie and Kelly Holmes.

▲ *Christine Ohuruogu holds up her Olympic 400 metres gold medal.*

The Olympic Games itself holds an important place in the history of race relations. At the 1936 Olympics held in Nazi Germany, Jesse Owens – an African American athlete – won four gold medals, disproving the Nazi belief in white supremacy. At the Mexico Olympics in 1968, Tommie Jones and John Carlos both gave the 'Black Power' salute on the medal podium to show their support for the Civil Rights Movement in the USA.

▶ *Jones and Carlos give the 'Black Power' salute at the 1968 Mexico Olympics.*

Did you know?

Now retired, superstar Michael Jordan has been called 'the greatest basketball player of all time'. He was also the highest paid in 1992 when he earned a $3.9 million salary from the Chicago Bulls, plus an estimated $32 million in endorsements from sports firms such as Nike. Jordan was responsible for popularising the US-based National Basketball Association (NBA) around the globe and is an inspiration to millions of people.

"Obstacles don't have to stop you," said Jordan. *"If you run into a wall, don't turn around and give up. Figure out how to climb it, go through it, or work around it."*

Sport and community

Today, black sportspeople are on equal footing with others, but this has not always been the case. In the past, important pioneers led the way to achieving a fair representation on the sports field. The experience of black sportspeople in overcoming prejudice has run parallel with the struggle to tackle discrimination in wider society, and sport plays an important part in bringing communities together.

Sporting equals

In 1948, the same year that the *Empire Windrush* arrived in England, black boxers were finally allowed to fight for the British title. Although the racial barriers that prevented participation in many sports have now largely come down, there are still issues that need to be tackled. In football, for example, black footballers playing for England have been racially abused by opposing fans. Fans at the Spanish Grand Prix also confronted Lewis Hamilton – the 2008 Formula One World Champion – with racist insults.

Sporting Equals was set up in 1998 by Sport England (with the Commission for Racial Equality) to promote the participation of ethnic minorities in sport and fitness. Its Racial Equality Charter encourages organisations to promote racial equality and quash discrimination. Coaching scholarships and mentoring programmes are part of its plan. The organisation also sponsors community projects, ranging from tennis and basketball, to African dancing.

▲ *Lewis Hamilton celebrates winning the Hungarian Formula One Grand Prix in 2009.*

Breaking the colour bar

After the end of the American Civil War, some African Americans played side-by-side with white sportsmen in integrated baseball teams. But in 1890, black players were unofficially banned from professional baseball and started forming their own teams. The first all-black team, the Cuban Giants, had been formed in 1885, and was followed by other new teams. From the 1920–1940s, the National Negro Leagues encompassed a nationwide network of all-black teams.

In 1947, baseball legend Jackie Robinson (1919–1972) was the first African American player to break the 'colour bar' when he joined the Brooklyn Dodgers, a white professional team. His success paved the way for other black players being accepted into Major League Baseball. Robinson was joined by Negro League stars Joe Black, Roy

▲ *Jackie Robinson playing for the Brooklyn Dodgers at Ebbets Field in 1947.*

Campanella and Don Newcombe, and by 1952, there were 150 black players in pro baseball. Black sportspeople could now play in the professional sports arena.

Did you know?

US boxer Muhammad Ali (right), was born in 1942. He changed the course of the sport when he became the only boxer to become world heavyweight champion three times: in 1964, 1974 and 1978. The outspoken 20th century icon has very definite views on identity:

"Hating people because of their colour is wrong. And it doesn't matter which colour does the hating. It's just plain wrong."

Tackling gang culture

Gang violence is a major concern in black communities in Britain and especially in the USA, where there is easier access to handguns. The police, parents and local organisations are all working to find ways to guide young people away from destructive gang culture and towards a more positive way of life.

Operation Ceasefire

In the USA, gang violence is a huge problem – and out of an estimated 772,500 gang members in 2000, almost one-third were African American. A number of police initiatives and community and church groups are tackling the problem. Operation Ceasefire, developed by the Boston Police Department, is considered one of the most successful anti-gang strategies. First implemented in 1996, police officers communicated to gangs that there would be quick and severe consequences for violence – such as lengthy prison sentences. The strategy worked: after one year, the number of gang deaths in Boston had dropped from 600 to 152. Ceasefire has since been used successfully in other US cities.

The Violence Prevention Institute in New Jersey hosts a number of programmes aiming to reduce youth violence through education and changing behaviour. It offers online resources for parents and schools. Homeboy Industries was founded by Father Greg Boyle in 1988 to tackle the serious

▲ Community police officers work towards changing behaviour, not just making arrests.

gang problem in Los Angeles, where 86,000 people belong to gangs. Fr Boyle believes that young people join gangs due to poverty, lack of education and lack of hope. Homeboy helps young people become contributing members of society through job training and shared community experience.

Mothers Against Violence

In the UK in 1999, an organisation called Mothers Against Violence was formed in Manchester after four shootings took place in one week, which led to the death of two people. Within a short space of time, M.A.V. had spread across other cities in Britain, including Nottingham, Birmingham, London and Leeds. The aims of M.A.V. include working with young people to encourage them not to carry weapons or join gangs, and helping them to find employment or training. Similar organisations have sprung up in black communities, trying to encourage young black people to move away from the temptations of gang culture. The From Boyhood to Manhood Foundation works with young boys in London who have been excluded from school and helps to build their self-esteem and confidence.

▲ *Training at a TV studio is one example of where young black men can learn job skills.*

Did you know?

• In the UK in 2007, it became illegal to sell knives to people under the age of 18 and it is illegal to carry a knife – if caught, you may face up to four years in prison and a £5,000 fine.
• Violent crime in the UK has fallen by 48 per cent since its peak in 1995.
• 11,789 people are killed by handguns in the USA each year; in England and Wales, 54 deaths per year are caused by handguns.
• In the USA, the majority of murder victims aged 12–17 are black.

The legacy of Rodney King

On the night of 3 March, 1991, African American Rodney King went on a drinking session at his friend's house in Los Angeles. He then got in his car, sped down the motorway, and was chased by a police car at 180 kph. Eventually, King was caught and while trying to resist arrest, was beaten severely by four police officers wielding metal batons. A local resident, George Holliday, caught the incident on video. The events that followed sparked a major race riot in Los Angeles.

The trial

Two days after Rodney King was beaten, George Holliday gave his videotape footage to a television station and it was broadcast on news shows across the country. Most people agreed that the police had used excessive force in restraining King, and the fact that four white men were thrashing one black man looked suspiciously racist. King was released from jail without any charges being pressed, and the police officers who beat him were put on trial.

The trial of the police officers was moved to an all-white district to influence the outcome. It began on 3 February 1992, with a jury of 10 white people, one Hispanic and one Filipino-American. The trial lasted until 3.15pm on 29 April, when the jury acquitted (found not guilty) three of the police officers and did not reach a verdict on the fourth. Los Angeles Mayor Tom Bradley said: "*The jury's verdict will not blind us to what we saw on that videotape. The men who beat Rodney King do not deserve to wear the uniform of the LAPD* [Los Angeles Police Department]."

LA riots

People were outraged at the result of the trial. The implication was that the LAPD was racist and that there was no social justice in America. At 5pm, rioting began on the streets of Los Angeles. Three days later, 53 people were dead, 7,000 people had been arrested and $1 billion worth of property was damaged.

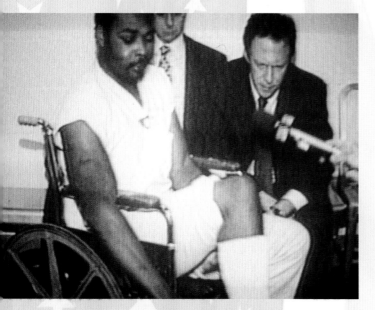

▲ *Rodney King appeared on TV soon after the attack, with bruises clearly visible.*

▲ Smoke rises from riots in Los Angeles following the result of the police trial.

In the midst of the rioting and looting, Rodney King made a press announcement in an attempt to calm the situation: *"People, I just want to say, you know, can we all get along? Can we get along? Can we stop making it horrible for the older people and the kids? It's just not right..."*

Aftermath

Following the riots, President George Bush Snr called for a Federal (national) trial of the officers for violating King's civil rights. Two of the police officers – Sgt Stacey Koon and Laurence Powell – were sentenced to prison for 30 months; the other two were acquitted. There were calls from the public for these sentences to be extended, but both men served their sentence and the case was closed. In 1994, King was given $3.8 million in damages from the city of Los Angeles.

Cultural impact

After the Rodney King case, several 'copwatch' organisations were formed. Founded in 1996, the October 22 Coalition to Stop Police Brutality aims to 'bring forward those most directly under the gun of police brutality' – this is most often people from minority groups, including African Americans. October 22 has been made a National Day of Protest to remind people of their civil rights. Another feature of the Coalition is the Stolen Lives Project, which documents cases of killings of citizens by law enforcement officers nationwide.

Stephen Lawrence

IN DEPTH

On 22 April 1993, Stephen Lawrence and his friend Duwayne Brooks, two teenage black boys, were waiting at a bus stop in Eltham, London when they were attacked by a gang of five white youths. According to Brooks, the gang made a racist comment before his friend was stabbed several times. Stephen died shortly afterwards from his wounds.

Lawrence inquest

The inquest that was held into the murder judged that Stephen was 'unlawfully killed in a completely unprovoked racist attack by five white youths'. The Metropolitan Police investigation into the murder, however, was not conducted properly and as a result, the charges that were brought against the five suspects were dropped. This meant that the Lawrence family had to bring a private prosecution in an attempt to get justice for their son.

But the private prosecution also failed – a judge ruled that the evidence provided by Duwayne Brooks was 'inadmissable' (which meant it wasn't reliable enough). Not long afterwards, the *Daily Mail* newspaper published a front-page article with the headline 'Murderers' featuring pictures of the five suspects. The *Daily Mail* challenged the suspects to sue the newspaper if the accusations were false. This has not happened, but to this day, no one has been found guilty of the murder of Stephen Lawrence.

▲ *The teenager, Stephen Lawrence, whose murder sparked a government inquiry.*

▲ *The* Daily Mail *newspaper followed the Stephen Lawrence case closely.*

The Macpherson Report

In 1999, the Home Secretary, Jack Straw, ordered a public inquiry into the case, which was carried out by Sir William Macpherson. The inquiry found the Metropolitan Police guilty of making a number of mistakes, including failing to provide Stephen with first aid, which might have saved his life.

The most important finding of the report was that the Metropolitan Police were guilty of 'institutional racism'. This meant that the police had failed to 'provide an appropriate and professional service to people because of their colour, culture or ethnic origin' as a result of discrimination due to 'prejudice, ignorance, thoughtlessness and racial stereotyping'.

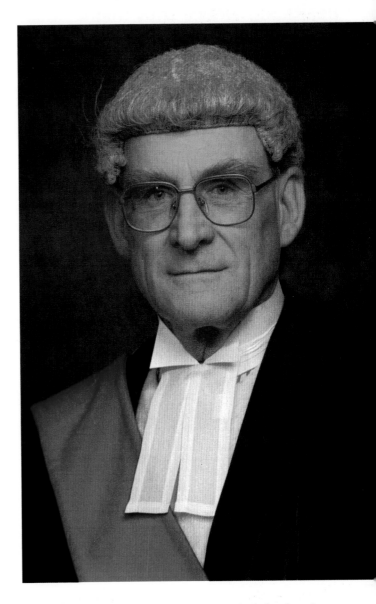

▲ *Sir William Macpherson, who led the inquiry into the murder of Stephen Lawrence.*

Black role models

Many people in black communities, the media and the government, have raised concerns at the lack of positive role models for young black people, especially men. In 2007 in the UK, the REACH project was launched to find 20 black male role models who would inspire a new generation. In the USA, initiatives from the NAACP and other organisations strive to place young African Americans in training positions, where they might become future role models themselves.

Reaching out

The REACH project, led by Simon Wooley of Operation Black Vote, Ozwald Boateng (a fashion designer), Tim Campbell (winner of *The Apprentice* TV show in 2005) and Leroy Logan (police superintendent), aimed to achieve two main objectives. First, they set out to

▲ *Black role models are important in many campaigns, such as this one fighting knife crime.*

'inspire young black men to be the best they can be; second, to encourage all black men to embrace their role as role models to their own children, and those of extended families'.

The 20 National Role Models have been chosen and range from Richard Reid, a firefighter from south London, to Alexander Beresford, a TV weather presenter. They will be visiting schools and youth clubs offering advice and encouragement as well as supporting mentoring programmes around the UK.

Leadership and higher education

Gateway to Leadership is a groundbreaking initiative from The Money Management Institute (MMI) and the NAACP. It hosts a summer internship programme that places outstanding African-American students from black universities in positions at some of the top US financial services

▲ *A student in New Orleans, USA, celebrates graduating from high school.*

The final frontier

Positive role models are emerging for young black women, too. Dr Maggie Aderin-Pocock MBE is a space scientist who builds satellites and is often seen in the media. As part of the annual National Science and Engineering Week, she has spoken to over 25,000 school children from all backgrounds about becoming scientists. "*Most of them are convinced that you need a brain the size of a small planet to be a scientist,*" she says. "*They generally think that we spring fully formed from white middle-class families, too. So I visit inner-city schools and take the students on my journey, telling them why I became a scientist.*"

firms. The aim is to provide real-world business experience, career counselling and mentoring, as well as to try to redress the minority balance – African Americans make up only 6 per cent of executives and managers in financial services.

A series of scholarship programmes also offer opportunities to African American students who want to go on to colleges and universities.

Diverse future

In the 20th century, immigrants from the Caribbean – and today from African countries – have changed the ethnic makeup of Britain forever. Many Africans have settled in the USA – arriving first as captured peoples and more recently as immigrants – to add to its fascinating blend of cultures. The challenge is to create societies where people from different backgrounds can celebrate their own heritage, while building an increasingly harmonious common culture with others.

Diverse society

With its quickly changing multi-ethnic society, Britain is facing up to challenges but is also enjoying new ideas. The sights, sounds, tastes and experiences that have been brought to the country by people of African and Caribbean heritage have added greatly to the UK's rich cultural mix. In the USA more than 200 years of African influence have enriched the culture, from styles of music that have become popular worldwide, to literature, sports, food, film and more.

▲ A crowd of cricket supporters in South Africa – bringing people from many communities together.

Identity and community

For many people, the question of identity is a complex one. Today, it is widely acknowledged that a person's identity consists of many aspects, ethnicity being just one of them. Community plays an important role in supporting people by providing them with a shared culture, history, language and set of morals and beliefs. While there can be

▲ *Multi-ethnic communities are exciting places to live, with diverse cultures.*

tension between those from different backgrounds, if there is an understanding of both similarities and differences, it is possible to work together to create a more peaceful society where people are united by the things they all have in common.

Who do you think you are?

John Henrik Clarke (1915–1989) was a writer, historian and pioneer in the creation of African studies. He wrote many books and articles, and edited anthologies of black writing. His lifelong quest for knowledge of his African identity began early: "*I saw no African people in the printed and illustrated Sunday school lessons,*" said Clarke. "*I began to suspect at this early age that someone had distorted the image of my people. My long search for the true history of African people the world over began.*" In 1986, the John Henrik Clarke Africana Library at Cornell University in New York was named in his honour.

Timeline – Community and Identity

1845 Frederick Douglass publishes his influential autobiography

1870 Hiram R. Revels represents Mississippi, becoming the first African American US senator

1904 Dr Alan Minns becomes the first black mayor to be elected to office in Thetford, Norfolk

1913 John Archer becomes the first black mayor born in Britain to be elected to office in Battersea, London

1947 Jackie Robinson joins the Brooklyn Dodgers

1948 *Empire Windrush* arrives in England with 492 migrants from the Caribbean. Black boxers were allowed to fight for the British title for the first time

1959 The first Notting Hill Carnival was held in St Pancras, north London

1965 The first UK Race Relations Act was passed, which made it illegal to discriminate on the grounds of race in public

1964 Muhammad Ali becomes world heavyweight boxing champion for the first time

1981 Race riots break out in London, Liverpool, Birmingham and Bristol

1987 Oprah Winfrey's show broadcasts across the US for the first time

1987 Diane Abbott, Bernie Grant and Paul Boateng become the first black Members of Parliament

1987 Black History Month becomes established in the USA, UK and Canada

1991 Rodney King is attacked by police officers in Los Angeles

1992 Michael Jordan reaches the height of basketball fame, becoming the highest paid basketball player

1993 Stephen Lawrence murdered in Eltham, London

1999 The Macpherson Report inquiry into the Stephen Lawrence murder case found the Metropolitan Police guilty of 'institutional racism'

2000 Race Relations (Amendment) Act passed, which made it necessary for public bodies to be proactive in tackling racial discrimination

2004 Kelly Holmes won two gold medals at the Athens Olympics

2005 Condoleezza Rice becomes US Secretary of State

2007 The Equality and Human Rights Commission was established

2009 Barack Obama is sworn in as the 44th US President

2011 Riots in the UK following police shooting of Mark Duggan

2012 Mo Farah a British Somali athlete wins double gold at the London Olympics

2014 Businessman Damon Buffini heads list of top black role models

Websites and Bibliography

Websites

http://www.history.com/topics/black-history-month
Website of the History Channel, featuring articles and lots of information and photographs to explore.

http://www.naacp.org
Homepage of the National Association for the Advancement of Colored People – includes information on current intiatives.

http://www.nabss.org.uk/
The National Association of Black Supplementary Schools.

http://www.sportingequals.org.uk/
An organisation that is committed to challenging racial discrimination in sport.

http://www.stephenlawrence.org.uk
The Stephen Lawrence Charitable Trust website, including information about bursary schemes and community action.

Bibliography

Carrington B & McDonald I, *Race, sport and British society*, Routledge, 2001

Dabydeen D, Gilmore J and Jones C (Eds), *The Oxford Companion to black British History*, OUP, 2007

Fryer P, *Staying Power, the History of black People in Britain*, Pluto Press, 1984

Holt R & Mason T, *Sport in Britain, 1945–2000 Making contemporary Britain,* Wiley-Blackwell, 2000

Forman M & Neal MA, *That's the joint!: the hip-hop studies reader*, Routledge, 2004

Majors R, *Educating our black children: new directions and radical approaches*, Routledge, 2001

Owusu K, *Black British culture and society: a text reader*, Routledge, 2000

Torrington A, *Windrush Pioneers*, Windrush Foundation, 2008

Glossary

Abolitionist
Someone who wanted to abolish the slavery of Black Africans.

Ancestor
Someone from whom you are descended.

Black Power
Beliefs and activities to increase the power of black people, especially in the USA.

British Empire
The United Kingdom and all the lands under its power that reached its largest extent after World War I.

Census
A population count.

Civil rights
The rights of all people to social and political freedom.

Colony
An area or country controlled by another country.

Colour bar
Preventing black people from doing certain jobs or activities with white people.

Community
A group of people living in a particular local area.

Culture
The arts, beliefs and traditions of a particular society.

Discrimination
Unfair treatment of a person or group because of their race, sex or beliefs.

Ethnic minority
A group that has a different racial or cultural background from most of the other people who live in a country.

Gangsta rap
A type of hip hop music. The words of the songs often reflect the violence of inner city life.

Homophobic
Holding negative feelings towards homosexuals.

Immigrant
Someone who moves to another country to settle.

Indentured servant
Someone who has signed a contract to work for a set amount of years in exchange for food, board and clothing.

Media
The name for newspapers, radio and TV.

Member of Parliament (MP)
An elected member of the House of Commons.

Migration
The movement of people from one place to another.

Mixed heritage
A person whose parents come from different racial groups. The father might be white British and the mother might be Asian or black British.

Multiculturalism
Relating to several cultures and the exchange of ideas between them.

Prejudice
An opinion or dislike formed against something or someone.

Race riot
A riot caused by hatred for people of other races living in the same community.

Racial discrimination
Unfair treatment of a person or group because of their race.

Role model
Someone whose behaviour or success can act as a good example to young people.

Segregation
Separation or isolation of a race of people from the rest of the community. In the USA this led to separate schools, restaurants and housing districts for black and white Americans.

Senator
An elected member of the US Senate (the upper house of the US Congress).

Sexist
Someone who believes that women are inferior to men.

Slavery
When someone is forced to work for another person and loses all of their freedom and rights.

Stereotype
A fixed idea of how something is or will behave – especially people.

Terrorism
The use of violence, or the threat of its use, in order to convey a political message.

Transatlantic Slave Trade
The name given to the enslavement and forced removal of millions of Africans from Africa to the Americas between the 16th and 19th centuries.

Index

Abbott, Diane 14, 16, 40
Aderin-Pocock, Dr Maggie 37
Africana 39
Ali, Muhammad 29, 40
American Civil Liberties Union 18, 19
Archer, John 14, 40

Black History Month 22, 23, 40
Boateng, Paul 14, 40
boxing 28, 29, 40
Boyle, Father Greg 30
Brooke, Edward 15
Brown, Carol Moseley 15
Bruce, Blanche 15
Bush, George W. 17, 33

Caribbean 9, 10, 11, 20, 22, 38, 40
Carlos, John 27
carnivals 8, 22–23, 40
Carver, George Washington 23
census 11
Christie, Linford 26
Civil Rights Movement 11, 17, 27
Clarke, John Henrik 39
Cole, Nat King 23
colour bar 29

Douglass, Frederick 14, 15, 40

education 11, 16, 17, 18, 20–21, 23, 30
Empire Windrush 28, 40

France 13
From Boyhood to Manhood Foundation 31

gangs 25, 30–31
gangsta rap 25
Gateway to Leadership 37
Grant, Bernie 14, 40

Hamilton, Lewis 28
Henry, Lenny 24
Holmes, Kelly 26, 40
Homeboy Industries 30

immigration 10–11, 12–13, 38, 40

Jamestown 10
Jones, Claudia 22
Jones, Tommie 27
Jordan, Michael 27, 40

King, Dr Martin Luther 11
King, Rodney 32–33, 40

Lawrence, Stephen 34–35, 40
laws (against racial discrimination) 11, 18, 20
leaders, community 14–15
London 14, 19, 22, 31, 40
Los Angeles 30, 32–33, 40

Macpherson Report 19, 35, 40
Mardi Gras 22
media 24–25, 36, 37
melting pot 12, 13
Members of Parliament (MPs) 14, 16, 40
Metropolitan Police 34, 35, 40
Minns, Dr Alan 14, 40
mixed heritage 9
Mothers Against Violence 31
multiculturalism 12–13, 38, 39
music 22, 23, 24, 25, 38

NAACP 18, 22, 25, 36, 37
Native Americans 10, 11, 12, 13, 22
New Orleans 22, 23, 36
Notting Hill Carnival 22, 40

Obama, Barack 9, 15, 40
Ohuruogu, Christine 26, 27
Olympics 26, 27, 40
Operation Ceasefire 30
Owens, Jesse 27

policing, community 30
politicians 9, 14–15, 16–17
Powell, Colin 17
prisons 18, 19, 30, 31

racial discrimination 11, 17, 18–19, 20–21, 22, 28, 35, 40
radio 20, 21, 24
REACH 36
Revels, Hiram R. 15, 40
Rice, Condoleezza 16, 17, 40
riots, race 19, 32–33, 40
Robinson, Jackie 29, 40
role models 14, 21, 24–25, 26, 36–37
'Roots' 24

Scarman Report 19
segregation 11, 15, 20, 23
senators, US 15, 40
Sentamu, Dr John 21
settlers, early 10, 12
slaves 8, 10, 11, 12, 14, 22, 24, 38
sport 24, 25, 26–27, 28–29, 38
Sporting Equals 28
stereotypes, media 24–25
stop-and-search 19

Thompson, Daley 26
Transatlantic Slave Trade 10, 12, 24

Violence Prevention Institute 30

Williams, Serena/Venus 26
Winfrey, Oprah 24, 25, 40

These are the lists of contents for the titles in *Black History*:

African Empires
Introduction
African Empires
Ta-Seti and Ancient Egypt
The Kingdom of Ta-Seti
Ancient Ghana
What was life like in Kumbi Saleh?
The Empire of Mali
Mansa Musa and the pilgrimage to Mecca
The Empire of Songhai
A rough guide to Timbuktu
The Kigdom of Benin
Living in Benin
Great Zimbabwe
Who built Great Zimbabwe?
The Europeans arrive
African resistance
A timeline of African empires
Websites and Bibliography

Africa and the Slave Trade
Introduction
Slavery around the world
West Africa at the time of the Transatlantic Slave Trade
The start of the Transatlantic Slave Trade
Britain and the triangular trade
Capture
Elmina
The Middle Passage
Olaudah Equiano
Arriving in the Americas
Sugar!
What was it like to work on the plantations?
What was it like to live on the plantations?
Mary Prince
How did enslaved Africans maintain their culture?
What was the legacy of slavery for Africa?
A timeline of the Transatlantic Slave Trade
Websites and Bibliography

Resistance and Abolition
Introduction
Resistance in Africa
Resistance on the slave ships
The Amistad
Resistance on the plantations
Slave revolts
Nanny of the Maroons
Toussaint L'Ouverture's rebellion
Abolition
Africans in Britain
Olaudah Equiano the Abolitionist
Society for the Abolition of the Slave Trade
Am I not a man and a brother?
The Abolition Acts
Elizabeth Heyrick
The legacy of the slave trade
Timeline – Resistance and Abolition
Websites and Bibliography

Civil Rights and Equality
Introduction
Nineteenth-century radicals
The Pan-African Conference 1900
John Archer
World War I
Race Riots
The League of Coloured Peoples
World War II
Windrush generation
Claudia Jones
Roots of the Civil Rights Movement
Martin Luther King and civil rights
The civil rights laws
The rise of Black Power
Race in the USA today
Race relations in the UK
Timeline – Civil Rights and Equality
Websites and Bibliography

Arts and Music
Introduction
The music of Africa
The impact of slavery
The actor – Ira Aldridge
The composer – Samuel Coleridge-Taylor
Images of black people in art
The Harlem Renaissance
The London scene
Writing in the civil rights era
Motown
Jimi Hendrix
The reggae beat
Dub poets
Punk and two-tone
From hip hop to dubstep
Contemporary artists, musicians and writers
Timeline – Arts and Music
Websites and Bibliography

Community and Identity
Introduction
Black Britons and African Americans
Multiculturalism
Community leaders
Diane Abbott and Condoleezza Rice
Flash points
Overcoming barriers
Celebrating black culture
Black people in the media
Sporting achievements
Sport and community
Tackling gang culture
The legacy of Rodney King
Stephen Lawrence
Black role models
Diverse future
Timeline – Community and Identity
Websites and Bibliography